MAY 2017

May
by the Bay

Anders Hanson

Consulting Editor, Diane Craig, M.A./Reading Specialist

Published by ABDO Publishing Company, 4940 Viking Drive, Edina, Minnesota 55435.

Printed in the United States.

Credits
Edited by: Pam Price
Curriculum Coordinator: Nancy Tuminelly
Cover and Interior Design and Production: Mighty Media
Photo Credits: AbleStock, Digital Vision, Wewerka Photography

Library of Congress Cataloging-in-Publication Data

Hanson, Anders, 1980-
    May by the bay / Anders Hanson.
        p. cm. -- (First rhymes)
    ISBN 1-59679-495-X (hardcover)
    ISBN 1-59679-496-8 (paperback)
        1. English language--Rhyme--Juvenile literature. I. Title. II. Series.

PE1517.H3765 2005
808.1--dc22

2005048785

SandCastle™ books are created by a professional team of educators, reading specialists, and content developers around five essential components that include phonemic awareness, phonics, vocabulary, text comprehension, and fluency. All books are written, reviewed, and leveled for guided reading and early intervention reading, and designed for use in shared, guided, and independent reading and writing activities to support a balanced approach to literacy instruction.

Let Us Know

After reading the book, SandCastle would like you to tell us your stories about reading. What is your favorite page? Was there something hard that you needed help with? Share the ups and downs of learning to read. We want to hear from you! To get posted on the ABDO Publishing Company Web site, send us e-mail at:

sandcastle@abdopub.com

SandCastle Level: Beginning

-ay

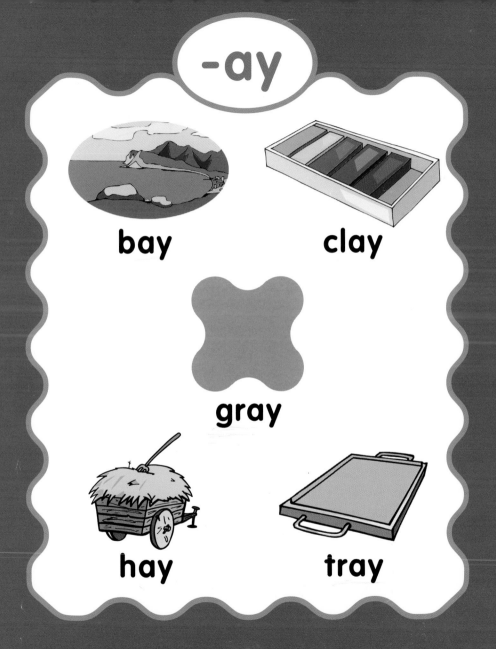

bay

clay

gray

hay

tray

Here is a  .

I look at  .

See the color .

I look at  .

Here is the .

The bay is big.

The clay is in a box.

Gray is a color.

The hay is yellow.

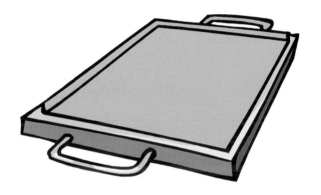

The tray is flat.

May by the Bay

May lives by the bay.

By the bay,
May likes to play
with her clay.

18

By the bay,
May puts some hay
into her clay.

May plays by the bay
and puts the clay
with hay out to dry
on a little tray.

At the end of the day,
the clay with hay
is gray.

May makes a raft
and sails away
in the bay.

About SandCastle™

A professional team of educators, reading specialists, and content developers created the SandCastle™ series to support young readers as they develop reading skills and strategies and increase their general knowledge. The SandCastle™ series has four levels that correspond to early literacy development in young children. The levels are provided to help teachers and parents select the appropriate books for young readers.

Emerging Readers
(no flags)

Beginning Readers
(1 flag)

Transitional Readers
(2 flags)

Fluent Readers
(3 flags)

These levels are meant only as a guide. All levels are subject to change.

To see a complete list of SandCastle™ books and other nonfiction titles from ABDO Publishing Company, visit www.abdopub.com or contact us at:
4940 Viking Drive, Edina, Minnesota 55435 • 1-800-800-1312 • fax: 1-952-831-1632